Surf Porn

gestalten

Exploring the Beauty of Surfing

Written by
Gaspard Konrad

Billions of years have passed since the first shores lined our planet, and still the waves persist in their ceaseless ballet, rolling in and out, each one unique. The earliest records of surfing date back to 12th-century Polynesia. Although surfing gear has undergone countless changes and updates since then, especially over the past 50 years, the allure of braving the waves on a surfboard remains the same to this day. The beauty of surfing is timeless. It is not just a sport; it is a way of life. It requires patience, practice, and dedication, but its rewards are priceless.

I first discovered my fascination with this incredible sport over 25 years ago, and since then, I've been steadily expanding my collection of extraordinary surf imagery. My Instagram account @surf_porn allows me to share these amazing images with the world. As you delve into the pages of this book, you will discover an unparalleled compilation of surfing and wave photographs that will leave you inspired. These exceptional shots, taken by my favorite photographers, combine unique angles and dramatic landscapes with a masterful use of light and color.

Unlike the high-performance action close-ups often associated with surf photography, the photographs in *Surf Porn* offer a more nuanced artistic perspective. They capture the ocean and the essence of surfing in all their glory.

I have chosen four main themes that, in my opinion, reflect the true spirit of surfing: exploration, self-expression, timing, and passion.

As surfers, we never stop chasing the perfect wave, the one we'll remember decades later. In search of untouched waves, the most passionate among us travel to the furthest corners of the globe. The whole world is our playground, with each continent, country, and wave offering its unique characteristics. The true essence of surfing is to leave behind the crowds and to seek waves off the beaten path. Enter the Spanish surfer-explorer Kepa Acero, whose journeys have taken him to some of the most secluded surfing spots in the world. Kepa is also passionate about sharing his memories of surf exploration with others, which makes him a perfect fit for this project.

Surfing is a display of strength, agility, and instinct. It holds profound spiritual significance; it is a thing of the heart. It is a communion and a dance with the ocean. The surfer's performance is fascinating: adapting to the wave, taming it, carving a path on it, forever in motion on this moving element. Surfing is a means of self-expression and a powerful mood booster—it never fails to lift your spirits. Torren Martyn, master of style and elegance, presents his point of view on this subject.

There's a consistent rhythm to the way the water moves, yet no two waves are the same. Timing is key. A perfect session is rare, but it is precisely this scarcity that makes surfing so intense and irresistible. A multitude of variables shape the magnificent experience of riding a wave, and that's why we come back to this sport time and time again. I asked Morgan Maassen to share his thoughts on the topic. Despite his young age, Morgan is fast becoming a legend in the field of surf photography. For him, timing is crucial not only for surfing but also for capturing those precious moments on the board with his camera.

Surfing is unlike any other sport. There are no quantifiable outcomes, no winners or losers. It's solely about pleasure, about finding joy in the great outdoors. Your surfing "success" can only be measured by the happiness it brings you. As the famous saying goes, "The best surfer in the water is the one having the most fun." Adrenaline rushes, breathtaking landscapes, catching the perfect wave... Surfing offers a potent mix of exhilaration and well-being. Lee-Ann Curren, a long-time surfer and European champion, was born into a family of renowned surf pioneers, including her parents and paternal grandfather. Her family background has undoubtedly nurtured her deep and unwavering passion for surfing. In this book, you will see how the push and pull of the surf shapes her life, our lives. Even when the ocean is entirely flat...

This book is a tribute to the beauty of surfing.

I hope it brings you joy.

Alan Van Gysen

Exploration

Written by
Kepa Acero

*"The swell is within me.
I am the storm.*

These words reverberate over and over inside me while I am here in this desert, far away from the rest of the world. Alone.

The bonfire has long since died down and the night is almost perfect at this hour. I say almost, because you are missing.

There is no light to mar the spectacular starry sky. The Milky Way beautifully illuminates the vast space above me. It is bright like a busy highway at night, the sole difference being that I am very far from the madding crowd. The only sound I hear is that of waves breaking on the shore.

I am camped in front of a cape that I discovered years ago on Google Earth, from the comfort of my couch, back home in the Basque country.

Since then, how often have I dreamed of being here, surfing the diagonal of this remote corner of Africa? Studying, day in and day out, the depth of the ocean, the direction of the swell, the wind, and the intervals between waves.

Google Earth's satellite imagery offered me a bird's-eye view of this place, but from such great heights, small details are rendered imperceptible. The colors of the desert, the sound of the wind, the smell of the sea.

Never could I have foreseen the setbacks I would encounter on my way here,

Anthony Fox

the difficulties I would have to face, the people I would end up meeting.

Uncertainty is the very essence of adventure, after all.

Imagine. Think. Perform.

Here I am, having waited so long for this storm to arrive! This swell I have been anticipating for years finally shows up in the forecast.

It has only just begun its journey from Antarctica and will take another week to reach this place, but at long last, the waves start to roll in.

They push ahead like solid walls toward our meeting point. On this shore, where I wait patiently, they will meet their end. Where my dreams are born, the waves die.

What impulse guides my journey? What mysterious magnetism pulls me toward this fleeting encounter with a wave? Sometimes I feel like a madman.

I could be at home, warm and comfortable with my girlfriend, listening to my father laugh while my mother cooks a delicious meal. I could be playing fetch with my dog.

Instead, I am alone in the desert, with this romantic dream of experiencing, if only for a brief moment, the boundless energy of the sea. All this just to be inside a wave for a few seconds.

Once again, I check the forecast and take a look at the traveling swell. I close my eyes and register the intensity of my emotions as I think of the storm. I make the swell mine; I feel that I am my waves, my oceans, and those words start to rumble all over again.

The swell is within me.
I am the storm."

This is an excerpt from a wanderer's journal I kept while exploring a remote part of Africa. Thirteen years have passed since I wrote these words and I have spent much time pondering what drives so many surfers to traverse the globe for a handful of waves.

The human condition is complicated. Many cultural, physiological, and social factors play a crucial role in how we make decisions, or choose one path over another.

However, after much consideration, I have come to the firm conviction that two of these factors define the experience of surfing: a profound connection with nature and what I call the "Wanderlust spirit." These remarkable features of surf culture flood the surfer's soul with dopamine—the "pleasure hormone" of the human brain—and inspire him or her to seek out the farthest reaches of our planet.

Surfing, a Profound Connection with the Natural Environment

A Peruvian friend whom I met in Chicama, Peru, once shared a beautiful story from the Mochica civilization with me. Back then, Chicama was a fishing village known as Mamape, which translates to "never-ending wave." Every morning, the men of the village would venture out into the sea in their small, narrow fishing boats. Upon their return, they would harness the force of the waves to propel their boats back to the shore.

One day, a 13-year-old boy accidentally caught a wave with his fishing boat, just as a surfer would on his board. Trying to escape the rolling waters, the boy found himself traveling at high speed. He would later say that gliding on the water made him feel as free as a pelican, and that he was eventually inspired to get up on his feet. He first pulled one leg up, then the other, and finally, he was standing upright, riding the wave. "I'm flying!" he yelled. From this day on, the boy spent all his time surfing.

Anyone who is familiar with the sensation of catching a decent wave knows the exhilaration this child must have felt in Mamape all those centuries ago—that feeling of a total lack of friction, of gliding in a perfectly smooth line. The sensation of flying. Once you experience various oceans and waves, you will understand that each corner of the world offers a unique adventure. Surfing lets you connect with the different parts of our planet in an intimate way. And most importantly, it is pure fun!

Chris Burkard

The "Wanderlust Spirit"

Over time, I have realized that a certain "Wanderlust spirit" has shaped the human experience since its very beginnings.

The etymology of this expression takes us to Germany, where it was especially popular among the Romantics. The German verb "wandern" means to travel on foot, while "Lust" equates to "lust" or "passion"—essentially, a passion for travel.

"Counterculture:" However, "Wanderlust spirit" is not only the thirst for adventure. Peope who embody the spirit are capable of facing their fears and of taking risks. Counterculture has always been an important part of surf exploration. The Beat Generation had a significant influence on surf culture, and in the 70s, countless surfers joined the ranks of those opposing the Vietnam War.

Many of these young rebels decided to travel the world in search of new waves. These restless souls were always thinking about their next destination, never knowing what adventures and human encounters lay ahead.

Circumstances change. So does technology. Humanity, however, stays the same.

In 2008, a new program called Google Earth pointed us toward one of the best waves on the planet, located in Namibia. The wave appeared in front of our eyes like our very own end of the rainbow. Many young people downloaded the app and began to dream of seeking out such a wave. Suddenly, maps had turned into so much more than color-coded political territories. We felt like majestic birds, soaring over the distant shores of the planet in search of a surfer's paradise.

We located new spots on the map, took our backpacks and surfboards. All that remained was to buy tickets and start following our dreams.

This is how we write the history of surf exploration. We honor the legacy of a counterculture that prioritized the ephemeral experience of riding a wave over the accumulation of material wealth, against all societal expectations. All we seek is the fleeting encounter with a wave, in a quiet corner of the world, with no other objective than to find pleasure and feel alive. Being exposed to new cultures, people, challenges, and ideas. In the end, what we gain is a deeper understanding of our own life experience.

Looking back at my diary entry from that night in the desert, I no longer believe I was a madman. I like to think that in that moment, alone and full of excitement, I was simply human. All I wanted was to live fully—nothing more, nothing less.

Kirvan Baldassari | ›› Alan Van Gysen

Luke Gartside

Chris Burkard

Dylan Gordon

Mark McInnis

Guy Williment | →→ Guy Williment

Self-Expression

Written by
Torren Martyn

Self-expression is an innate part of being human, and for surfers, it takes on a unique significance through our deep connection with the ocean and Mother Nature.

I've always found it hard to express myself with words, and that's where I've found surfing to be an outlet. I've been lucky enough to spend much of my life traveling in search of waves, and I've had some incredible and profound experiences along the way.

Last year, somewhere off the coast of Sumatra, I came across what turned out to be one the most memorable surfs I've ever experienced. We had started our sailing trip as total novices, and it had been a wild and daunting three-month journey all the way to Indonesia and its surfable waves. I had loved the challenges of learning to sail, but it had also been stressful and all-consuming. We had finally made it to an island chain with abundant waves, and I was feeling a sense of accomplishment and relief that we had arrived in one piece. On that particular day, my friend Ishka and I woke up early and set out on the dinghy. We wanted to look at a bit of reef that had swell wrapping around it, not quite sure what we were hoping to find. The state of the ocean seemed unreadable, but the first set wave that wrapped itself around this particular corner of the reef in front of our eyes was completely mind-boggling. As the day progressed and the sky cleared, the

ocean came alive. This fickle and unfamiliar part of the reef produced some of the best waves I had ever seen. There was no one else around, apart from us and little *Calypte*, our sailboat, which was bobbing offshore, near a small, deserted island. I remember sitting in the lineup, in between waves, and thinking that I had everything I could ever want or need. I was so grateful to be there and felt overwhelmed by happiness. It is through surfing that I have truly experienced the feeling of being completely in the moment. It has pushed me out of my comfort zone and has also become the place where I feel the most comfortable.

I love that through surfing we not only connect with nature, but also develop a deeper bond with ourselves and the people with whom we share this profound experience. Surfing—if we let it—allows us to disconnect from the stresses and pressures of the world and be present. We use the ocean and the waves as a means of expression, letting our moods, emotions, and experiences shape the way we ride and perceive the waves.

For me, traveling in search of waves is one of the most enriching and incredible experiences I can imagine, not just for the surf itself, but also because of the journey along the way. A few months ago, I sat on the deck of the *Calypte* on night watch. It was 2 a.m.; no one else was awake—just the sounds of the rigging creaking and gentle waves hitting the hull of the boat. Phosphorescent algae lit our path, illuminating the bow. As we floated along over thousands of square feet of water, the stars reflected off the glassy ocean surface, and it felt like we were drifting through space. In the silence of that moment, I felt self-reliant in a way that I had never experienced before. The solitude and the wholeness of the moment were very freeing. There's a real softness to being out there on watch. It feels like you could be the only person left in the world, and nothing else matters. Living on the boat, immersed in moments like these, taught me new ways of seeing myself and understanding the world.

Riding a variety of boards, and sailing too, has taught me new ways of expressing myself as I move through life. I've found that riding different surfboards enables me to surf different parts of a wave and experience different feelings. This simple principle has reminded me of the importance of trying unfamiliar things, or taking new routes and risks to reinvigorate old pathways. In the last year, sailing has been a novel and extremely rewarding outlet for me. I've learned to see the ocean differently, and it has renewed my appreciation for wind and weather patterns. Sailing has become a fresh approach to interacting with the ocean and has taught me a lot of respect for the power of the elements. I've become interested in boat design as a medium to harness winds and currents and move through the ocean in new ways.

Surfing can take us to some of the most remote and breathtaking places on Earth, where we encounter new cultures, new smells, sounds, and landscapes, and meet other surfers from around the world. It requires a thirst for adventure, an open mind, and a willingness to step out of our comfort zone. And when we return home, wherever that may be, we are able to bring those experiences and those memories with us.

Throughout our lives, we weave our way through different chapters, influenced by different people, places, and the experiences we collect along the way. From surfing perfect waves in exotic locations to witnessing stunning natural phenomena, these memories shape us as individuals and give us a broader perspective on the world around us. They ultimately help us to create and inspire our own paths. For me, surfing has been the truest form of self-expression. Through my relationship with the ocean, and the many journeys I've embarked on in search of waves, I have deepened my relationship with myself and forged many beautiful connections, both with other people and with the natural world.

Luke Gartside | ↦ Tom Hawkins

Tom Hawkins

Tom Hawkins | →→ Anthony Fox

Tom Hawkins

Timing

Written by
Morgan Maassen

I would argue that timing is the most fascinating component of surf photography.

Timing is such a complex and nuanced element of surfing. As surfers, we're always chasing something: wind, swell, waves, conditions, tide, light, uncrowded wilderness. And as surf photographers, we're chasing those factors to capture the feeling, the sense of achievement, that comes with the experience. This is why most surf photographs are not of perfect waves; rather, they're extraordinary attempts to chase that sensation we seek.

To search for waves, to relish the sense of achievement that comes with surfing, one must be at peace with what lies at the heart of surf culture: the unknown.

We can, however, juggle all of the aforementioned factors and strive to do our best, which reduces the chance of failure and magnifies the great beauty of chasing surf. I've been a surfer for over 20 years, and taking up the challenge of surf photography has been the honor of a lifetime. It's my attempt to do justice to and document our dance with the ocean.

Navigating our lives is always complicated, but when we're left to the whims of the wind and the sea, surfing can feel both like a source of frustration and a game of chance. I could write a book about the school days I spent absorbed in my studies, when outside the surf was perfect. And then there were the lazy weekend days I idled away,

waiting for the fog to lift or a ripple of swell to appear. "This is the surfer's conundrum!" everyone laughs, as girlfriends grow angry and massive obligations are weighed against a potential hour of surfing in average conditions.

I sometimes loathe surfing, for I wish it was as easy as skateboarding: board meets concrete. Accessible whenever there's no pouring rain! Or think of tennis, where courts are always available! But then I look at the world surfing has opened up to me, from the lush jungles of Brazil to the scorching desert of Australia to the sparkling reefs of Reunion Island. I've met best friends, broken more than one bone, been chased by sharks, slept in airports, drunk from waterfalls, and worn the same clothes for a week straight. I've traversed the globe for perfect waves and turned up empty-handed, and I've met people in a pub who took me to the best surf of my life the next morning, less than a mile away from a place where I would have given up in defeat.

These moments are magical and priceless. They built me, and in turn I built a body of photographs and stories that can span 10 lifetimes. I've learned to live by the creed, "treasure the hunt," as there is often great disappointment when you set foot on the beach and take in the waves you thought you were chasing. In these travels, enjoying the people and wildlife and nature and adventure, I've found my treasure. The journey for surf is everything, the experiences you gather along the way the ultimate reward. These days, when I look at tennis courts I shudder at their simplicity, at how little adventure they offer—and I love playing tennis.

As I've navigated the great defeats and struggles of wave hunting, dealing with so many variables at once, both my appreciation and endurance have increased exponentially. I am more grateful for the doors that open along the way, but I also probe at them. The fisherman at the harbor or the mysterious sign on the road may guide us to a wave or beach that we previously overlooked. Taking time and enjoying the solitude and beauty of such an endeavor has led me to be patient enough to actually wait out the perfect moment. I'm now an (almost) professional weatherman, sailor,

hiker, camper, chef, travel agent, even astrologer. I lose sleep at night as my brain decodes what the ocean will do next, and how I can anticipate it. I traverse land, sea, and sky with utmost efficiency to chase down moments that I need to experience and capture.

Timing can be defined by three pillars: skill, preparation, and opportunity.

Several years ago, I saw a perfect wave break out to sea in northern Australia, as a storm moved in and engulfed it in rain. I sat in my car, constantly buffeted by the downpour, eating power bars, double- and triple-checking forecasts and tides and weather readings. I waited for days to capture the shot I wanted, sunrise to sunset. I would pop out of the car, document the jungle, beaches, and people, cherish sunny moments in which I could swim, or climb the rocks near my camera and just…wait.

Days later—I was tired but not defeated—the moment finally came.

The rain had subsided, and as I peered through the window, I saw another storm mounting behind a flawless wave. Climbing to the ideal perch on the headland, I got my photograph of the perfect wave, as it was swallowed whole by a rainstorm. The image shows the barrel with not a drop of water out of place, and the dark-blue sea blending into the sky as the heavens release a torrential waterfall (p. 129).

I ran back to the car, elated. Days of work and patience had been poured into this single moment. For the first time, I asked myself what had been the purpose of all this. I hadn't even surfed the wave. Frankly, it wasn't surfable: it was half a mile out to sea, surrounded by sharks, and breaking with far too much power for my skill level or the equipment I had brought with me.

It wasn't about the ride—it was about the moment. Capturing it, experiencing it. That wave was unattainable, but it was everything to me. Beauty, perfection, a dream.

144 Anthony Fox | ← ← Guy Williment | Alex Postigo

← ← Luke Gartside | Kirvan Baldassari

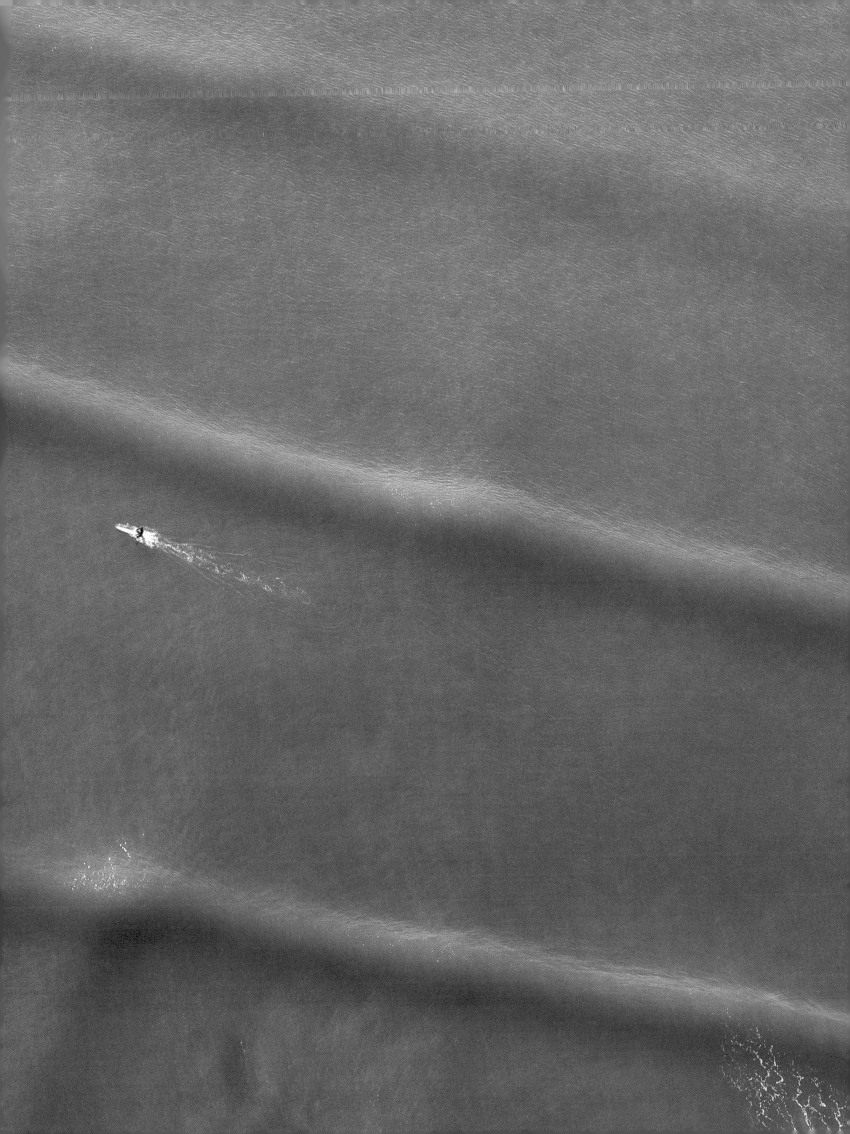

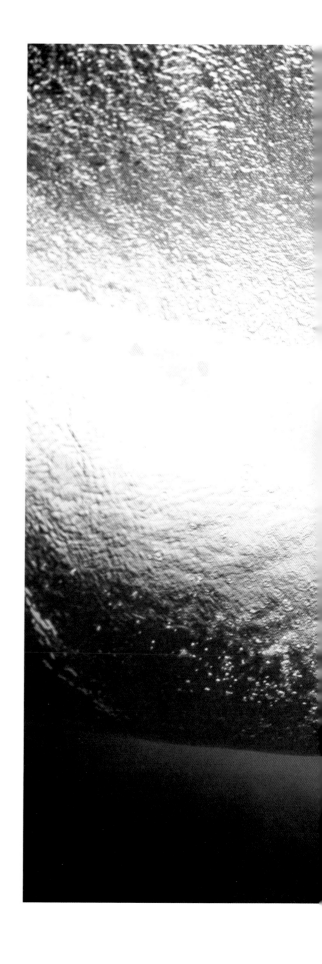

Anthony Fox

Helio Antonio

Arenui Frapwell

Morgan Maassen

Sébastien Picaud

Ed Sloane | ✦ Mike Coots

Passion

Written by
Lee-Ann Curren

It's been flat for 6 months.
I haven't been surfing.

My skin is recovering, my hair has stopped splitting at the ends, and my eyes are no longer dry. I hear sounds clearly, without the crunchy distortion I'd grown so used to.

My brain operates more quickly, and it's taken some time to adjust to its new pace. My ideas are precise, abundant, not fuzzy. I feel like a normal person now. I've accepted my new reality.

A flat ocean is a different beauty. It's peaceful. I can swim to the rocks out at sea; I can take things slow. I can lie on a towel and get a real tan, not just the signature surfer's crest (tanned from the collarbone upwards). I can read a book or complete a sudoku.

Looking at the ocean has become restful; it's one big, sparkly mass of blue, green, and gray now. I don't need to endlessly analyze its movements, or guess what's happening underwater between the sandbars and rocks. I don't need to predict what would happen if the tide were to change. No more surfing every single wave in my mind, no pointing at every amazing ride that I might be missing out on, no more "ohhhh"s and "ahhh"s and grimacing in anticipation.

All the surfboards have been mended and freshened up; they are resting in sheds, or decorating walls. In some backyards, you will still find chunks of the old, gray wax, forgotten in a corner. Surfers have started cleaning their houses, no longer spending all their energy out in the water,

and most beachfront homes now display a level of feng shui that wouldn't look out of place on the pages of *Dwell* magazine.

My body is thanking me. I feel rested, and my mind is at peace. It's a relief not to be plotting the next surf. I no longer keep tabs on surfing conditions along the entire coastline; I don't care about crowd movements and weather patterns across all of France, Europe, or the Earth at large. I don't need to monitor traffic flow or tide changes and plan my life accordingly. I'm a reliable person. I have time to sleep. All I do is sleep.

I haven't been cutting my nights short to catch the sunrise, to gaze at the ocean and marvel at the simple magic of waves making their final, graceful arrival on shore after a very long journey.

There have been no 5 a.m. alarms and no long drives to see it all come together: the sun climbing up behind the sand dunes and over the pine trees, with the gentle and cold easterly wind pushing straight against the swell lines, mixing the smells of resin and ocean spray, shaping waves hollow and perfect, brushing their hair back in a glorious swoop.

We used to take our time, establish a game plan, carefully pick the right board. We'd wonder whether we could reach the calm beyond the breakers, and we'd always take the chance, butterflies in our stomachs, rosy-cheeked.

One of us would catch the first wave and disappear under the lip, and the rest of us would cheer. Paddling over a set and catching a side view of the wave curling, the image of the lip instantly freezing in memory, reflecting light in all directions, almost crystal-like.

It became a dance, and we paid for our mistakes with stiff necks, or a little sand in our ears, or the heartbreak of watching a wave roll on without us.

We'd see the light move through the turning waters and feel the board glide ever so smoothly over the surface. We'd apply the right amount of pressure at just the right part of the rail, and we'd be propelled at infinite speed to places we'd never dreamt of going. Sometimes, for a split second, time would stop.

It was a dance of falling, getting back up, adjusting, and trying again, and again, and again. It was beautiful, silly—it didn't have to make sense.

Now, the music has stopped.

My nerves tingle as I picture all this, and feelings begin to flood in. I may have gotten used to this dull face, these soft feet, and this greasy skin, but this, too, is just a phase. Maybe I should check up on those boards in the shed, see if they're still there. Maybe I should start getting into shape again.

When the flat spell comes to an end, we will be shadows in the dark again; we'll meet at the end of my street before dawn breaks, filling the car with boards and rubber, water and snacks. Up to no good, strategizing how to outsmart the crowds, we'll drive through the night and dive into cold waters. We'll go to the places no one else dares to go. Bones will grow in our ears, and wrinkles will draw lines around our eyes.

After a day in the ocean, we'll put on our stupid grins, satisfied at last. Our thoughts will be fuzzy. Our hearts will drum to the same beat.

Stu Gibson

Chris Burkard

Alex Postigo

Sébastien Picaud | ▸▸ Luke Gartside | ▸▸▸ Dylan Gordon

Kepa Acero

Spain

The legendary Spanish surfer embodies the true essence of adventure and passion. Kepa has dedicated his life to searching for new waves, and his relentless pursuit of the unknown has led him to fearlessly explore remote surf spots across the globe. Wherever he goes, Kepa carries a heart full of love and a smile that lights up the world. His inspiring journey continues to inspire our own adventurous souls!

Morgan Maassen

USA

Born with an innate talent and a love for surfing, the Santa Barbara-based photographer transports us to a world where surf and art collide. With a keen eye and a deep connection to the waves, Morgan's work transcends the realms of photography. His images are like visual poetry, painting the beauty and power of surfing in vivid colors.

Torren Martyn

Australia

The enigmatic surfer embodies the true spirit of surfing. Hailing from Australia, Torren Martyn is known for his soulful approach and unique style in the water. His love for the ocean runs deep, and his connection with the waves is nothing short of poetic. Whether he's gliding gracefully across long peelers or fearlessly charging heavy barrels, Torren's surfing is a captivating display of skill and grace.

Lee-Ann Curren

France

Coming from a family of surfing legends—her father is the renowned surfer Tom Curren—Lee-Ann has carved her own path with remarkable style and finesse. A former European surfing champion, Lee-Ann is now shifting away from professional surfing to become a free surfer. Off the board, Lee-Ann's creative spirit shines through various artistic endeavors. As a musician, producer, filmmaker, and visual artist, she explores different facets of her creativity.

Surf Porn

Surf Photography's Finest Selection

This book was edited and designed by gestalten.

Contributing editor: Gaspard Konrad
Preface by Gaspard Konrad

Edited by Robert Klanten

Text by Kepa Acero (pp. 6–10), Torren Martyn (pp. 72–74),
Morgan Maassen (pp. 128–131), and Lee-Ann Curren (pp. 197–199)

Editorial Management by Anna Diekmann
Design and Layout by Joana Sobral
Cover by Stefan Morgner
Photo Editor: Madeline Dudley-Yates

Typefaces: Nysé by Stéphane Elbaz and Futura Std by Paul Renner

Cover image by Mike Coots

Printed by Schleunungdruck GmbH, Marktheidenfeld
Made in Germany

Published by gestalten, Berlin 2023
ISBN 978-3-96704-128-6

FSC
www.fsc.org

MIX
Paper from
responsible sources
FSC® C105039